home decorating workbooks

wreaths and garlands

home decorating workbooks

wreaths and garlands

Paula Pryke

photography by James Merrell

RYLAND
PETERS
& SMALL

First published in Great Britain in 1998
by Ryland Peters & Small
Cavendish House
51–55 Mortimer Street
London W1N 7TD

Text copyright © 1998 Paula Pryke
Design and photographs copyright ©
1998 Ryland Peters & Small

Produced by Sun Fung Offset Binding Co., Ltd
Printed in China

ISBN 1 900518 64 3

A CIP catalogue record for this book is available
from the British Library.

Creative Director **Jacqui Small**
Publishing Director **Anne Ryland**
Series Art Editor **Paul Tilby**
Series Editor **Zia Mattocks**
Project Art Editor **Colin Walton**
Project Editor **Bella Pringle**
Art Assistant **Sailesh Patel**
Production **Meryl Silbert**
Illustrator **Helen Smythe**
Stylists **Martin Bourne**
Margaret Caselton
Nato Welton

contents

Throughout the world, in every culture, circles, rings, wreaths, garlands, and swags of fresh and dried plant materials have always been steeped in symbolism and meaning. The wreath, in particular, has come to signify eternal love, friendship, remembrance, and even life itself. At both religious and secular events, these decorations have had a role to play—floral headdresses were worn by both bride and groom as a symbol of purity, and flower garlands were, and still are, offered as a greeting to guests in many countries.

Although the craft of wreath- and garland-making dates back to ancient Greece and Rome, it is still popular today, having never really disappeared from our collective experience. By weaving flowers into wreaths, we are continuing a long tradition of designing circular forms for healing or spiritual well-being as well as for their own esthetic value.

Contemporary wreaths, garlands, and swags are essentially flower arrangements without containers and are designed to be displayed on or around doors or walls, draped around parasols and table edges, or worn as headdresses by brides and bridesmaids. Whatever its intended location or use, the modern wreath most commonly maintains its traditional circular shape, but can also be in the form of a heart or novelty shape, and is often associated with remembrance and respect for the dead. Garlands of flowers and foliage, on the other hand, have happier associations. These long, flexible floral decorations are suspended horizontally or vertically from architectural or garden features.

Large-scale garlands of fresh flowers are curled around pillars, tent poles, or staircase banisters for dramatic effect, or hung in dainty chains around a table edge. Swags are typically vertical hanging decorations, but they tend to be shorter and more compact than garlands. Often swags are simply hand-tied bunches of flowers that rely on the plant stems for support rather than being attached to a rigid or flexible wreath base.

The true craft of wreath-making is taking whatever is plentiful and inexpensive in nature and fashioning it into an imaginative decoration. Take pleasure in collecting objects, such as pebbles and driftwood from the seashore, and enjoy the fact that each new season brings fresh materials for wreath-making. Even before I worked professionally with flowers, I took great delight in making fresh and dried displays from mushrooms and moss and other plant matter that I gathered on woodland walks. I also relished the fall, when I could create simple wreaths out of autumn leaves. These displays were not extravagant or beautifully constructed, but there was a sense of achievement in making my own decorations for the home.

Although the following pages are full of inspirational ideas and projects, I hope you will look upon them as a starting point for your own designs. I came to floristry after a career in teaching history and never considered myself artistic. Now that I work with flowers every day, I am constantly amazed at how each individual brings his or her own feel and look to a display even when starting with identical materials. I think the secret of success is having the confidence to express your style. It is also important to plan the display to suit its location. Whether fresh or dried, wreaths and garlands are the most beautiful natural embellishments we can bring into our lives. They are timeless art forms that we can make for ourselves and our friends.

Paula Pryke

room decorations

Festoons of flowers, foliage, herbs, and fruit were first brought into the home to celebrate harvest and to dry and store seeds; they are one of the earliest forms of floral display. Later, swags of decorative fruit and flowers became popular architectural details in room interiors and were carved from stone or wood or molded from plaster. Today, the use of fresh wreaths as room decorations has undergone a revival—they are used to stunning effect as door, wall, and table ornaments.

above Freeze-dried roses and bunches of dried lavender and marjoram make up this long-lasting, scented display. The heart-shaped base is cut from dry floral foam, wired to a pole and inserted into a pot packed with dry floral foam. *left* A cornucopia-shaped basket is decorated with sun-dried seedheads and strands of snake grass. A plastic container of water is set into the basket and filled with crown imperials to produce a colorful door decoration for a party.

above and right These attractive paper flowers and dried and dyed red maize were bought from Native Americans in Arizona. I have attached these treasures to a twig wreath sprayed blue as a reminder of the use of color in the Southwest.

opposite top left Crab-apples last well in displays. Here, they have been wired to a dry floral foam ring, to offer a warm welcome at a fall gathering.

opposite top center Adapt an old wreath frame to create a living wreath of fresh green baby's tears plants. To do this, remove the foam, drill drainage holes in the base, and fill with soil and plants.

opposite top right Hydrangea flowerheads turn burgundy in the fall. Packed into a floral foam ring, they dry naturally to form a permanent display.

left Twig wreath bases provide the foundation for many fresh floral displays. Here, small vials of water are wired to the base to keep bachelor's buttons and scabious alive. Trailing ivy hides the base, and shells add interest.

below For a modern Shaker-style decoration, simply cut Styrofoam™ into three star shapes and glue red mung beans onto each one. Hang the stars from red ribbon on wooden coat pegs.

seashell and starfish wreath

This permanent wreath design introduces a nautical theme to bathroom decoration. Select a mixture of mother-of-pearl, scallop, oyster, clam, and spiral shells in a variety of shapes and sizes, and juxtapose their intricate patterns and smooth finishes with spiky, textural starfish and coils of heavy-duty rope.

materials & equipment

2 circular wire frames, 30-inch diameter

10 yards rope, 2-inch diameter

4 pieces driftwood, 16 inches long

6 mother-of-pearl shells • 2 yellow clam shells

3 cream conch shells • 7 brown-and-white striped conch shells

9 pearl-white spiral cones • 7 long brown spiral cones

4 oyster shells • 1 brown-and-white spiky shell

5 large brown mussel-type shells • 5 large cream mussel-type shells

11 large starfish • 11 small starfish • 8 fan-shaped scallop shells • selection of small shells

spool wire • wire cutters • scrap paper • silver spray paint • hot glue gun and glue sticks

instructions under flap ➤

everlasting heart of roses

A delicate heart-shaped wreath covered in freeze-dried red roses and sprigs of dried purple lavender makes an eye-catching wall display. Freeze-drying is a specialized technique that preserves the natural beauty of the rose petals; the dried roses do not become brittle and disintegrate, but look spectacular for months to come.

materials & equipment

heart-shaped straw wreath, 18 inches across at widest point

1 yard deep purple rope, ½-inch diameter

3 yards red burlap ribbon, 3 inches wide

25 bunches dried lavender (*Lavandula*), 5–8 stems per bunch

46 freeze-dried roses (*Rosa*)

30 preserved galax leaves (*Galax*)

spool wire • wire cutters • glue • floral scissors • medium-gauge floral wires

instructions under flap ➤

1 Place one circular wire frame on top of the other. Bind the two frames together with spool wire to make an extra-strong base to take the weight of the rope and shells. Lay the double frame on scrap paper, spray it with silver paint, and leave it to dry.

2 Hold one end of the rope and start coiling it loosely over the wire frame counterclockwise; the rope should encircle the frame at least four times.

3 Arrange the coils of rope on the frame and, when you are happy with their position, use spool wire to bind the rope to the frame.

4 Evenly space the four pieces of driftwood around the wreath and then glue them securely into place on the rope.

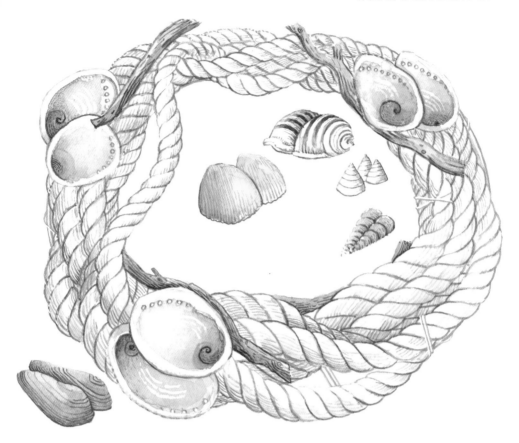

5 Decide which point is the top of the display, and then start gluing the larger shells onto the rope. Arrange the shells in pairs or groups of three, and try to balance the colors and shapes around the circular display.

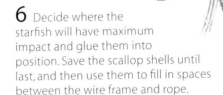

6 Decide where the starfish will have maximum impact and glue them into position. Save the scallop shells until last, and then use them to fill in spaces between the wire frame and rope.

7 Hide any sections of the wire frame that are still visible by gluing small shells onto the frame in groups. When the glue is dry, hang the wreath on the wall from a sturdy nail.

horseshoe of succulents

A symbol of good luck in many cultures, the horseshoe is an attractive shape for this wreath created with a variety of succulent species. These popular house and garden plants are ideal subjects for "living wreaths," since they need only small quantities of water to survive once their roots are embedded in a damp mossy base.

materials & equipment

¼-inch chicken wire, 1 x 4 feet

damp sphagnum moss

plastic bag

30 mixed succulent plants (*Echeveria*)

floral scissors • spool wire • wire cutters

U-pins • medium-gauge floral wires

instructions under flap ➤

gardening-theme wreath

For the gardening enthusiast, a wreath decorated with seed packs, scarecrow dolls, gnomes, flowerpots, watering cans, and other novelty items makes an original and personal gift. Hung on the shed or kitchen door, it will be a constant source of delight throughout the gardening year.

materials & equipment

circular twig wreath, 20-inch diameter

1 stem honeysuckle vine (*Lonicera*), approximately 10 feet long

dried carpet moss • 5 novelty watering cans

5 small terracotta flowerpots • 2 miniature fences

4 pieces driftwood, 6–8 inches long

garden trowel and fork

3 yards beige burlap ribbon, 2 inches wide

10 dried mushrooms • 5 packs of seeds

3 garden gnomes, 3½ inches tall • 4 scarecrow dolls, 3½ inches tall

spool wire • medium-gauge floral wires • wire cutters • glue

instructions under flap ➤

driftwood frame

Wood gnarled and bleached by the sun adds a primitive beauty to any room interior, and here, a rectangular wire frame offers a rigid base on which to show off these driftwood treasures. The beauty of this arrangement is that it is simple and inexpensive to produce and works well as a unique and eye-catching detail. Half the fun of this creation is collecting the material from a park or seashore and piecing together this woody jigsaw puzzle.

materials & equipment

rectangular wire frame, 24 x 18 inches

8 large pieces of driftwood

40 driftwood twigs

1 large, flat pebble

fine-grit sandpaper

spool wire • wire cutters

natural string • scissors

hot glue gun and glue sticks

instructions under flap ➤

silk-covered button ring

Put your sewing skills to the test by creating this striking purple silk ring studded with an assortment of buttons. Inspired by the fruit and vegetable sellers of London, England, known as the pearly kings and queens, who were famous for decorating their clothes with a lavish collection of pearl buttons, this wreath is both rich and textural.

materials & equipment

circular twig wreath, 22-inch diameter

2 strips heavyweight (8-ounce) batting, 14 x 70 inches, joined end-to-end

purple raw silk, sufficient for a strip 15 x 70 inches

200 buttons in a selection of colors, shapes, and sizes

1 yard red rope, ½-inch diameter

scissors • needle • straight pins

purple thread plus an assortment of other colors

instructions under flap ➤

above Sprigs of mistletoe are wired into damp sphagnum moss in two hanging baskets to make this traditional kissing ball.
left Corn is an important symbol in Thanksgiving celebrations; here, dried cobs are tied with raffia to a circular twig frame.

seasonal wreaths For thousands

of years, the variations in flowers, fruits, and foliage

available at different times of the year have been used to

mark the great seasonal events. In the winter months, pine

and mistletoe are abundant and form the backbone of

Christmas displays, while golden corn and wreaths of

leaves celebrate the fall. In spring and summer, the wealth

of fresh flowers available produces stunning floral displays.

opposite top Shimmering gold
and purple ribbon and fruits
decorate this blue fir wreath.
top of page Preserved magnolia
leaves maintain their glossy dark
green sheen and distinctive shape
and look stunning on their own in
a classic-style wreath.

center left A snowflake frame of
blue fir is simple to make; just wire
six plant stakes together with
spool wire at the center point.
bottom left Make a "living
wreath" by binding potted plants
to a frame. These miniature roses
take pride of place on a wall.

above These mixed colored
ranunculi, with their dark centers,
are one of my favorite flowers
because of their cheerful faces.
Bind the stems with rope and pack
them in water covered by sacking.
Tie them to the gate to indicate
where the party is being held.

candle centerpiece

Candlelight adds to the special atmosphere when you entertain outdoors. Here, a mosaic-style hurricane lamp is encircled by a rich mix of indigo delphiniums, and purple bluebells and anemones, offset by white ranunculi and starflowers, and green guelder rose and ivy to make a striking centerpiece. By covering the candle with a hurricane lamp, you can keep the flame alive in a breeze and prevent molten wax from dripping over the flowers and table.

materials & equipment

glass mosaic hurricane lamp and votive candle

circular floral foam base, 15-inch diameter

6 stems fruiting ivy (*Hedera*), 2 groups of 3

9 sprigs guelder rose (*Viburnum opulus*), 3 groups of 3

14 purple anemones (*Anemone coronaria*), 2 groups of 7

8 white ranunculi (*Ranunculus*)

10 starflowers (*Ornithogalum montanum*), 2 groups of 5

10 blue delphiniums (*Delphinium* 'Blue Bees'), 2 groups of 5

10 bluebells (*Scilla*)

floral knife • floral scissors

instructions under flap ➤

sunflower garland

For a special summer party, decorate a parasol with swags of vivid yellow sunflowers and yarrow, red chili peppers, and soft green scented herbs, bound onto a length of garden string. While this garland is simple to make, the choice of plant material is important because the flowers and foliage must be able to survive out of water without drooping. For a longer-lasting garland, attach the flowers and foliage to a damp moss or presoaked floral foam base.

materials & equipment

for a parasol with an 8-foot diameter, you will need to make a garland
24 feet long; make it in eight separate 3-foot sections.

for 3 feet of garland:

10 sunflowers (*Helianthus*)

12 sprigs fruiting ivy (*Hedera*)

17 clusters red ornamental chili peppers (*Capsicum*)

10 stems dill (*Anethum graveolens*)

7 yellow yarrow (*Achillea* 'Moonshine')

12 pincushion protea (*Leucospermum cordifolium*)

garden string • floral scissors • spool wire • wire cutters • needle and thread

instructions under flap ➤

ring of autumn leaves

Rich red and orange beech leaves, preserved in glycerin, are used to construct a glowing autumnal display. This method of drying plant material captures seasonal colors and prevents dried leaves from becoming dull and brittle. Available from specialized florists, glycerinated leaves look stunning for six months or more.

materials & equipment

for a 20-inch diameter wreath:

30 stems honeysuckle vine (*Lonicera*), 65 inches long

20 branches preserved beech leaves (*Fagus*)

floral scissors • spool wire • wire cutters

medium-gauge floral wires • heavy-gauge floral wire

instructions under flap ➤

christmas wreath

Extend a warm welcome to guests during the festive season by decorating the front door with a Christmas wreath. The custom of bringing greenery into the home dates back to pagan times, when evergreen was brought inside for the winter solstice. Here, soft branches of blue fir entwined with shimmering gold ribbon, small cones, and clusters of cinnamon sticks and dried orange slices release a heady mix of spicy and pine-scented aromas.

materials & equipment

circular wire frame, 17-inch diameter

sphagnum moss • plastic bag

5 branches blue fir (*Abies nobilis*)

gold cherub

6 dried orange slices

6 pine cones

24 cinnamon sticks, 6 groups of 4

¾ yard blue ribbon, ⅛ inch wide

2¾ yards gold ribbon, 2 inches wide

spool wire • wire cutters • floral scissors • U-pins

medium-gauge floral wires • heavy-gauge floral wires

instructions under flap ➤

left Roses and sprigs of skimmia make a perfect scented hanging ball for a special party or wedding. Make the ball by cutting a block of wet floral foam to shape. Attach a cord around the center of the foam and insert the skimmia and roses. Handle the rose heads with care to avoid bruising the petals.
below Sweet-scented stephanotis has been wound around a circle to produce a dainty bridesmaid's ring.
bottom of page Fragrant herbs and flowers are wired onto a small bridesmaid's basket filled with candy to offer to guests.
opposite, top of page Richly scented blue hyacinth bulbs are planted in a wire frame that has been filled with soil and covered with carpet moss to hold moisture within the wreath.

scented wreaths

Bringing flowers, leaves, roots, and bark into the home to fill each room with fragrance has always been popular; the original scented wreath for the home may have been a circle of bay leaves, sacred to the Greek god Apollo. Choose flowers and foliage to grow in the yard for their fragrance as well as their appearance and carefully select the plant materials you bring indoors. Silver foliage plants such as blue fir or eucalyptus, with their fresh woody scent, work well, as do richly fragrant flowers such as hyacinths, stephanotis, roses, and lilies, whose heady scents will linger in the room.

above A star-shaped wire frame is covered with moss and sprigs of fragrant blue fir to create a welcoming Christmas wreath.

left Silver-gray eucalyptus pods are bound to a circular frame using spool wire. The fragrance of the buds can be very strong, so the wreath is best hung outside so as not to be overpowering.

heart of fresh roses

A heart-shaped foam base, available ready-made from floral foam manufacturers, is the perfect frame for a delicate display of fragrant pale pink 'Anna' roses and lacy white hydrangeas that makes a romantic token for a summer wedding party. Suspend the heart from a length of green velvet ribbon for the finishing touch.

materials & equipment

heart-shaped floral foam base, 17 inches across at widest point

20 inches green velvet ribbon, 1½ inches wide

30 pink roses (*Rosa* 'Anna')

27 sprigs guelder rose (*Viburnum opulus*)

6 hydrangeas (*Hydrangea macrophylla*)

floral knife • heavy-gauge floral wire • floral scissors

instructions under flap ➤

personalized gardenia display

White gardenias are one of the most exquisite of scented plants and are popular with brides the world over. Their creamy flowers and waxy foliage make elegant displays with a wonderful perfume. A personalized decoration such as this, in the shape of an initial or number, would be perfect for a birthday, wedding, or anniversary.

materials & equipment

floral foam designer board, 12 x 20 inches

square pot, 8 x 8 inches, 10 inches high

wooden pole, 20 inches long • 4 handfuls gravel

2 stems clematis vine (*Clematis vitalba*), approximately 4 feet long

scrap paper • gold spray paint

4 medium-sized gardenia plants (*Gardenia*)

pencil and paper • floral knife

floral tape • medium-gauge floral wires

wire cutters • floral scissors • pebbles

instructions under flap ➤

wreath of lilies and apples

I enjoy using fruit and flowers together, and here, crisp green apples and beautiful scented white lilies offer a fresh lime-green mix of plant material. The white lilies sit on presoaked floral foam blocks, but even so, the display will have a limited life, because the wired apples release a natural gas that ages plant material.

materials & equipment

circular honeysuckle vine wreath, 22-inch diameter

carpet moss

3 small dome-shaped blocks of floral foam with screw-in bases

18 green apples

9 sprigs fruiting ivy (*Hedera*)

3 white hydrangeas (*Hydrangea*)

2 pure white lilies (*Lilium* 'Casa Blanca')

6 white lilies with creamy yellow centers (*Lilium* 'Pompeii')

3 strands trailing ivy (*Hedera*), 8–12 inches long

medium-gauge floral wires • floral scissors

instructions under flap ➤

opposite top left Red ornamental chili peppers are wired onto a single-wire wreath frame. Arrange the stalks end-to-end for variety and pack them tightly to conceal the wire base.

opposite top right Store garlic in the kitchen by attaching raffia to the stalk of each garlic bulb and threading the bulbs onto a twig frame. Garlic cloves can be cut off as required for use in cooking.

opposite below Small apples are wired to a moss frame by threading a floral wire through the apple flesh and twisting the ends together. Leaves and skimmia flowers help conceal the moss.

below Terracotta pots filled with herbs and tied together with rope make a decorative roof-top display for the urban gardener.

above Flowers and foliage can be used to decorate baskets of food for a party. Here, ivy and poppies are threaded through a twig basket filled with dried fruit and nuts. Wash foliage carefully when using it to decorate food.

right Choose a strong-headed flower such as marguerite daisies to make a garland of flowers around a table. Thread the back of each flowerhead onto a length of spool wire for a summery look.

above A star-shaped wire frame has been covered with ¹/₂-inch chicken wire, tied to a pole, and cemented into a pot. Spray the star gold and then leave it to dry while you tie ribbons onto candy wrappers. Then attach the candy to the wire to cover the star.

right An assortment of fun, brightly colored sticks of candy and lollipops have been tied with ribbon to a simple twig wreath for a children's celebration.

culinary themes

Foods, particularly breads, have long been associated with wreaths. The Egyptians fashioned bread into rings as a form of payment before the introduction of money, while in Greece, the family makes a circular wedding bread to symbolize well-being and good fortune. Above all, culinary wreaths are a useful and attractive way to store ingredients such as chili peppers, garlic, and candy, while food baskets and dessert tables look wonderful draped in flowers and foliage.

citrus-fruit ring

Groups of wired-up fresh oranges, lemons, and limes surrounded by sprigs of dark evergreen fruiting ivy leaves and berries make a striking winter wreath of natural ingredients. The fruit adds texture, color, and scent to the display at a time of year when flowers and foliage are in short supply. Place this brightly colored centerpiece on your dining room or kitchen table as an imaginative alternative to a traditional bowl of winter fruits.

materials & equipment

circular metal frame, 16-inch diameter

sphagnum moss

80 bunches fruiting ivy (*Hedera*)

15 lemons • 15 oranges • 15 limes

spool wire • wire cutters

plastic bag • U-pins

medium-gauge floral wires

floral scissors

instructions under flap ➤

grape and cherry garland

For summer buffets, a garland of fruit and edible nasturtium flowers around the dessert table makes a fresh and colorful addition. Dainty garlands such as this can be simply constructed on a thin gold cord and pinned to the tablecloth. First wash the materials, especially nasturtiums, to make sure they are bug free.

materials & equipment

the length of rope and quantity of fruit, nasturtiums, and ivy will depend on the size of your chosen table; for a table 24 inches in diameter allow:

2¼ yards gold cord, ½-inch diameter

5 strands of trailing ivy (*Hedera*), 20 inches long

2½ pounds green and black grapes

2½ pounds cherries

6 packs edible nasturtiums (*Tropaeolum*)

floral scissors • floral tape

pearl-headed pins • medium-gauge floral wires

instructions under flap ➤

eggplant and orchid wreath

The striking contrast of deep burgundy eggplant and anthuriums set against vivid yellow pattypan squashes and yarrow produces a richly exotic table display. The flowers and foliage are grouped together for maximum visual impact and interwoven with swirls of stephanandra stems to create movement.

materials & equipment

circular wire frame, 18-inch diameter

sphagnum moss

9 anthuriums (*Anthurium*)

30 baby eggplants

2 stems stephanandra vine (*Stephanandra tanakae*), 3 feet long, leaves removed and reserved

10 sprays yellow yarrow (*Achillea* 'Moonshine')

15 orchids (*Cymbidium*) • 30 yellow pattypan squash

spool wire • wire cutters • floral scissors

U-pins • heavy-gauge floral wires • medium-gauge floral wires

instructions under flap ➤

above To create a token of your love on Valentine's Day, soften red dogwood stems by soaking them in warm water and bend them into a heart. Secure the shape with red ribbon and two 'Grand Prix' roses.

above A heart-shaped frame, packed with damp moss and covered in soft lilac and pale green hydrangeas, stunning yellow 'Sultan' gerberas, and 'Golden Gate' roses, makes a dazzling display for a golden wedding.

celebrations
Since ancient Greek and Roman times, people have chosen wreaths and garlands to celebrate great events. The Greeks crowned the winners of their poetic and athletic competitions with garlands of fresh laurel, oak, and olive leaves, while the Romans chose head wreaths to honor their great military heroes. What better way to mark a special occasion, whether it is Valentine's Day, Christmas, or an anniversary, than by following in this grand tradition and creating a memorable display of flowers or foliage?

above A hand-tied posy adds the finishing touch to a church event. For impact, mix soft green lady's mantle and pink hydrangeas with deep red peonies, cockscomb, and 'Black Velvet' roses. Here, the flowers were threaded through an iron ring candle holder on the cross to hold them in place.

above Constructed from plant stakes held together with spool wire, this eye-catching gold star is covered in hundreds of tiny oak leaves. Each leaf has been dried, sprayed gold, and then glued onto the stakes. Hide the framework by making sure that the gold oak leaves overlap one another.

above A trailing swag of ivy and butcher's-broom foliage are mixed with lilac, hyacinths, ranunculi, and spires of bell-shaped campanula to produce a fragrant display. A fresh floral foam dome, which clips onto the rounded arm of the church pew end, forms the foundation for this diamond-shaped arrangement.

above A spectacular Christmas
wreath is created using a whorl of
birch twigs dipped in red paint
and sprinkled with glitter. To shape
the birch twigs into a ring, cut the
stems to 3 inches long and bind
groups of birch twigs to one
another with spool wire. Bend the
twigs into a circle as you work until
the ring is complete. Tiny lights are
threaded through the birch at the
back of the wreath to make the
display sparkle, and the cord is
hidden from view.

left A hanging festive wreath of
bright flowers and candles is built
up from a wire-frame foundation
covered in moss. The candles and
curls of ribbon are then attached
to the base with heavy-gauge
floral wires before the display is
hung. Once in location, fruiting ivy
and sea holly form a bed of foliage
for vivid marigolds, 'Jaguar' roses,
ranunculi, and anemones.

bridal headdress

This dainty spring headdress looks charming on small flowergirls, young brides, or girls taking their First Holy Communion. Constructed on a fine wire frame so it is light to wear, it can be tailor-made so it fits comfortably. The flowers and foliage, including delicate lilies-of-the-valley, hyacinth flowerets, purple-edged ranunculi, and small-leaved ivy, come together to impart a deliciously subtle fragrance.

materials & equipment

15 sprigs ivy (*Hedera*), plus individual leaves

11 lilies-of-the-valley (*Convallaria majalis*)

15 blue hyacinths (*Hyacinthus*)

15 fritillary (*Fritillaria pinardii*)

16 blue bachelor's buttons (*Centaurea cyanus*)

10 white lisianthus (*Eustoma grandiflorum*)

11 variegated ranunculi (*Ranunculus* 'Cappuccino')

fine-gauge floral wires • silver wire • wire cutters • floral tape

large circular tin • medium-gauge floral wires • floral scissors • pliers

instructions under flap ➤

heart-shaped table centerpiece

Tall displays of flowers and foliage, either incorporated on a candelabra or, as here, elevated on a pole, have become increasingly fashionable for the guest tables at weddings. Not only do they make a theatrical impact in a large room, they allow guests to witness the speeches without anything obstructing their view.

materials & equipment

stone urn, 18 inches high, 12-inch diameter

2 blocks floral foam, 8 x 4 x 3 inches

heart-shaped twig wreath, 10 inches across at widest point • sphagnum moss

1-inch chicken wire, 1 x 3 feet • wooden pole, 32 inches long

15 sprigs beech foliage (*Fagus*) • 15 sprigs lady's mantle (*Alchemilla mollis*)

15 sprigs pittosporum (*Pittosporum*) • 15 sprigs guelder rose (*Viburnum opulus*)

13 mauve hydrangeas (*Hydrangea*) • 14 blue scabious (*Scabiosa*)

16 pink lisianthus (*Eustoma grandiflorum*) • 15 pale pink roses (*Rosa* 'Delilah')

strand of ivy (*Hedera*), approximately 30 inches long

plastic bag • floral knife • floral tape • floral scissors

wire cutters • spool wire • heavy-gauge floral wires

instructions under flap ➤

chair-back decoration

This simple hand-tied swag of scented pink roses and rich purple lisianthus is easy to make and looks stunning. Use a generous length of brightly colored satin ribbon to attach the swag flamboyantly to the back of the chair where a guest of honor will sit, or make several to decorate the aisle seats at a wedding.

materials & equipment

1 yard raffia

5 stems viburnum (*Viburnum tinus*)

16 deep pink roses (*Rosa* 'Martinez')

9 pale pink roses (*Rosa* 'Delilah')

4 cockscomb (*Celosia argentea*)

18 purple lisianthus (*Eustoma grandiflorum*)

4 yards cerise ribbon, 2 inches wide

floral scissors

instructions under flap ➤

banister garland

Create a grand staircase for your guests by constructing an abundant garland of fresh flowers and foliage on a floral foam base. The foam foundation can be bought in standard lengths from specialized florists and joined together to achieve the desired length. Presoak the foam base to keep the fresh materials well-watered, and take care to fasten the garland securely to the banister, since the finished display will be very heavy.

materials & equipment

floral foam garland, available in 6-foot lengths composed of 6-inch sections;
for each 6-inch section you will need approximately:

20 sprigs dusty miller (*Senecio cineraria*)

4 green double lisianthus (*Eustoma grandiflorum*)

4 pink double lisianthus (*Eustoma grandiflorum*)

2 white tuberoses (*Polianthes tuberosa*)

2–3 cream roses (*Rosa* 'Anna')

10 sprigs snowberry (*Symphoricarpos*)

1 yard satin ribbon, 1¼ inches wide

plastic sheets • floral scissors

spool wire • wire cutters

instructions under flap ➤

wreath materials

Wreath frames can be purchased from good florists, garden centers, and specialized floristry suppliers, and are available in an extraordinary variety of shapes and sizes. Made from natural materials such as flexible dogwood stems, honeysuckle, or clematis vine, and bound together with spool wire or garden string, these simple rigid foundations form the building blocks of fresh or dried flower displays.

A purchased wreath base is always a worthwhile investment because, unlike fresh floral foam bases, they can be reused again and again. However, if you want to create a particular shape it may be simpler and more cost-effective to create your own base. Amateur gardeners or enthusiastic walkers can collect plant stems and trailing vines from the yard or countryside to fashion into wreath bases. Select any pliable woody stems and try to harvest these branches in spring before

the sap rises, or in the autumn after the sap has fallen. Dogwood, corkscrew hazel, and birch are my favorite woods, and honeysuckle, kiwi, wisteria, and grape are my favorite garden vines, but you can also find clematis and honeysuckle in the wild. If the twigs or vines are dry, soak them in warm water until they become more flexible and easier to work with. Start by picking out a few long stems and gently ease them into a circle. If the stems are too short, keep adding new lengths by staggering and overlapping stems until you have a circle. Bind the stems tightly with spool wire as you work to keep the twigs in place. The wire can be removed when the stems are dry, if they have taken on the right shape.

WREATH MATERIALS

wire frames

Rigid wire wreath frames can be purchased ready-made in a bewildering number of dimensions. There is little standardization for popular shapes, such as crosses, circles, and stars, since manufacturers from different countries have their own sizing systems based largely around funeral wreath traditions.

If you cannot buy the size or shape of frame you require, you could try making your own, but bear in mind that it may be difficult to buy materials such as floral wires, spool wire, and other sundries in small quantities. Most florists will carry a limited stock, but they may be reluctant to sell them to the

public, and they may have to order them specially from wholesalers. For a more "do-it-yourself" approach, try molding wire coat hangers into simple heart-shaped frames or folding a length of chicken wire around a strip of damp moss and bending it into a shape. Of course, medium-gauge floral wires and silver wire form the underlying structure for lightweight bridal headdresses, but for sturdier metal-framed structures, you could commission a metal worker to solder iron into the required shapes.

Wire frames are more permanent than either twig or foam bases and can be used again and again. Often damp moss is attached to the bare wire frame with spool wire to form a moist bed for fresh flowers. If the moss is very damp, the back of the wire wreath can be lined with plastic to protect the surface.

large-scale designs

Wire frames are ideally suited to particularly large and heavy displays. For grand-scale designs, two wire frames can be bound together with spool wire to reinforce the structure; sturdy wire frames are used to support a large nautical-theme wreath constructed out of twists of rope and shells (see page 12) and a heavy frame of driftwood (see page 28).

floral foam bases

Fresh floral foam is green, and dry foam is either brown or gray. Both types of foam come in blocks or specially molded shapes; fresh foam is soaked in water before use to prolong the life of the flowers and foliage. Inserting stems into moist foam will help plant materials stay fresh for longer, although they will not last as long as they would if arranged in a vase of water. Although fresh floral foam bases are simple to work with, they are really suitable only for short-term hanging decorations, because as the foam dries out and contracts, the plant material becomes dislodged and drops out. For this reason, foam shapes are best used for table centerpieces; the foam sits in a plastic base that protects the table surface. When soaking a fresh floral foam block in water, allow the foam to sink gradually. When air bubbles no longer rise to the surface, it is ready for use. Bear in mind that fresh foam can be used for only one fresh-flower display, since it will take up water effectively only on its first soak.

Although there are only a few floral foam manufacturers, the styles and shapes of the products they offer vary enormously. By ordering supplies from mail-order catalogs, you can select the sizes and dimensions you wish, as good

florists and garden centers hold only limited stock. In addition to round ring frames, balls, cones, and open-heart shapes, there are flat designer boards that can be cut into any shape. Also, specialized foam designs can be purchased for keeping fresh flowers and foliage alive on twig and wire wreaths. One type consists of a small block of dome-shaped floral foam held in a plastic cage with a screw-in base. Another type, designed to attach fresh flower displays to church pews, consists of a similar dome with a removable attachment that clips onto the pew end.

flexible bases

Flexible foam bases, which can be draped along a banister, are also available for creating garlands out of delicate plant materials that require a constant supply of water to prevent them from wilting. These specially manufactured floral foam bases can be bought in 6-foot lengths, divided into sections, and must be soaked thoroughly in water before use.

equipment & techniques

wreath-making equipment

A flat, non-scratch work surface that stands at a suitable height so the user does not have to stoop is the first piece of equipment needed for wreath-making. It is also useful when creating hanging wreaths to have a place where you can hang the display so you can check how the finished arrangement will look. Scrap paper on the work surface and drop cloths on the floor are also essential, especially when you are working on a display on location. Opt for plastic rather than fabric drop cloths to prevent moisture from seeping through to the floor or carpet below. When you have finished, you can simply fold up the ground sheets to clear away any waste material.

essential tools

Floristry scissors and shears are essential for collecting fresh plant materials and cutting stems. A small floral knife is handy for stripping the lower leaves from stems and for trimming blocks of floral foam to shape. Wire cutters are required for cutting chicken wire and floral wires, and pliers are useful for closing up clasps on headdresses. A glue gun is an indispensable tool for those who enjoy attaching unusual and heavy items, such as shells and wood, to wreaths, but should be used with care. The hot liquid glue adheres most materials, including wet items and dry porous objects, and it saves time, as it takes only a few seconds for the glue to dry. Both high- and low-temperature guns are available; low-temperature guns are more suitable for attaching fresh plant material, which can scorch on exposure to heat. Waterproof floral tape is also useful for anchoring wet foam blocks in containers, as is gutta-percha tape, which seals moisture within plant stems.

conditioning plants

The most recent research recommends the following simple guidelines for conditioning fresh flowers and foliage before they are arranged on a wreath. If you follow these measures

and condition flowers and foliage for several hours or overnight, they will last longer in the finished display. As a general rule, take at least 1¼ inches off the bottom of the stem and make a slanted cut with a sharp floral knife to expose the maximum surface area to water, rather than smashing or splitting the base of the stem. Next, remove the lower leaves from the plant stems, because leaves submerged underwater may rot and produce bacteria that will shorten the life of the plant material. Before placing the cut flowers and foliage in a container for conditioning, make sure that it is scrupulously clean and fill it with fresh lukewarm water, mixed with flower food. The food will feed the flowers, promoting longer life, and will prevent bacteria from growing.

protecting surfaces

It is a good idea to protect doors, walls, and tables, or any other surfaces or items of furniture in the home that may come into contact with water or moisture from fresh flower wreaths or garlands. Water is particularly harmful to unprotected wood finishes and can leave marks that are difficult to remove or cause the wood to warp. For small table wreaths, simply place a waterproof table mat or piece of thick felt under the tablecloth, but for grand-scale designs that are too large to sit on a mat, you will have to make your own protective covering out of a waterproof material. The best method is to cut up a plastic bag into long thin strips and fasten the strips to the back of the wreath with U-pins to prevent dampness from penetrating the furniture or wall.

Pin several strips of plastic over the damp moss covering the wreath base to prevent any water seepage.

To make a solid double-sided heart-shaped base for fresh flowers, fill the center of an open heart-shaped twig wreath with damp moss or presoaked floral foam blocks; then wrap it in a sheet of chicken wire and fasten the edges with lengths of spool wire.

small amount of color fading. When the materials are thoroughly dry, store them in large cardboard boxes or paper bags. Make sure that the flowers or leaves do not touch one another and place them between layers of tissue paper to avoid damaging the plant material. Avoid using plastic bags, as they become moist and cause the dried flowers and leaves to deteriorate.

adapting wreath bases

If you cannot find the exact wreath base for your project, adapt the materials you have at your disposal and make your own. For example, if you want to create a heart of fresh flowers, fill an existing heart-shaped twig frame with damp moss or blocks of presoaked floral foam and sandwich the moss or foam within the frame with chicken wire. Remember, most materials can be cut or trimmed to shape to suit your needs. For example, presoaked floral foam can be tapered to fit

drying your own materials

If you wish to create more permanent wreaths, buy bunches of dried materials, such as roses and glycerinated beech leaves, from a good florist, or try harvesting and drying your own materials, such as roses from the yard. In recent years, there have been great improvements in the quality of dried flowers available for purchase, mainly due to new techniques for freeze-drying flowerheads, particularly roses. These new methods have produced amazingly lifelike flowers whose petals maintain their natural beauty and suppleness. However, displays using freeze-dried flowers must be kept away from moist conditions, such as those found in kitchens and bathrooms, because the flowers tend to absorb moisture from the air and deteriorate rapidly.

The simplest way to dry your own plant materials for wreath-making is to hang them in bunches and store them in a cool, dark, dry room. If you have a warm, dry closet with enough space, use it as a drying area. Warm air will dry plant materials quickly, with only a

One of the simplest ways to create an attractive wreath base is to apply small dabs of hot glue from a glue gun to the underside of a ribbon; the glue dries instantly to hold the fabric in decorative folds on the wreath base.

any container and then held in place with waterproof floral tape, and flat designer board can be cut into a letter or number, using a template as a guide. Twig and dry foam bases are even more versatile than floral foam and form the foundation for many displays; they can be used time and again to different effect. A twig frame makes a good starting point for a fabric wreath—wrap the frame in quilted material to create a padded effect, then cover it in the fabric of your choice. Alternatively, natural wreath bases can be coated with spray paint.

attaching materials to wreath bases

The stems of fresh flowers and foliage are easy to insert in a fresh foam base, but there are several tried-and-tested techniques for attaching materials to dry foam or twig bases. Objects such as ribbon and shells are best glued to the base using a hot glue gun or strong adhesive, while groups of decorative items, such as dried fruits and cherubs, should be wired to the wreath or pinned securely in place.

Two standard blocks of floral foam are used to make a base for fresh flowers and foliage in a stone urn. The urn is lined with plastic before the presoaked blocks are added, their edges tapered to shape with a floral knife.

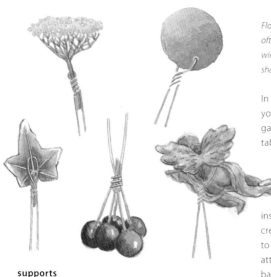

Flowers, leaves, fruit, and other decorative objects are often wired on a "double-leg mount," whereby a single wire is threaded through the item, bent into a hairpin shape, and the "legs" of wire twisted together.

In addition to attaching plant materials with wires, you can also use pearl-headed sewing pins to fasten garlands of flowers and trails of ivy and fresh fruits to tablecloths for special celebrations.

using rope, ribbon, or raffia

The great choice of colorful ropes, ribbons, and raffias available to the wreath-maker is inspiring, and these materials will add the finishing creative touch to any display. Use your imagination to explore their use on wreaths, and experiment by attaching pleated folds of pretty ribbon to a wreath base with a hot glue gun or pinning a length of luxurious velvet or silk ribbon to a wreath frame to make a decorative hanging for the display. Alternatively, attach the ribbon after all the other materials have been added, wrapping trails of ribbon around the flowers and foliage, and finishing off with a bow. Colorful paper raffia can also be used to bind together hand-tied swags of flower stems that are then attached to a chair back with a generous length of ribbon and finished with a double bow.

maintaining the finished wreath

Once you have created your wreath, garland, or swag of fresh flowers and foliage, keep it looking its best by spray-misting the plant materials and moss base with clean water on a daily basis. If the materials have been conditioned well beforehand, they should last for several days to a week within the display. For arrangements built on a foundation of fresh floral foam, keep checking that the foam is moist to the touch and add water only when it starts to dry out. For more long-lasting displays, choose plants that thrive on little water, such as succulents. These fresh displays will last for up to six weeks and are known as "living wreaths." To keep wreaths of dried flowers and foliage in good condition, keep them out of moist environments that may cause the plant materials to deteriorate. Try also to keep them away from direct heat and sunlight, which makes plant materials fade, and dust them at regular intervals to prevent dust particles from collecting on leaves and petals.

supports

Wire is essential in wreath-making for holding the structure together, for anchoring a bed of moss to the wreath base, and for attaching decorative plant materials, fruits, objects, and ribbon bows. The two main types of wire used are floral wire and spool wire. Floral wire comes in a bewildering number of thicknesses and lengths, and its primary function is to reinforce the plant stem. As a general guideline, use fine-gauge floral wires to support delicate flowers and leaves and to wire up individual flowerets in bridal work. Medium-gauge floral wire is used to support medium-sized flowers and decorative objects, while heavy-gauge wires are reserved for large or heavy flowerheads or to create a hook to hang the finished wreath. Spool wire is useful for all kinds of binding work. It is used to bind flexible twigs and vines into wreath frames, to attach moss and heavy decorative items such as rope and driftwood onto purchased frames, and to bind individual stems and bunches of flowers and foliage onto a length of rope to make a garland. In addition to using these wires, you can also use U-shaped pins to fasten materials to a wreath base. These work particularly well if you want an item to sit flush with the frame, for example, clumps of carpet moss or branches of pine, or when you are attaching a waterproof backing to a wreath. Either buy U-pins from specialized suppliers, which can be prohibitively expensive, or make your own by cutting heavy-gauge floral wires into short lengths and bending them into shape with pliers.

A decorative bow is easy to make: simply fold a ribbon into three loops and pinch the loops together in the middle. Take a second length of ribbon and tie it in a single knot around the center of the loops.

plant directory

Abies nobilis (**blue fir**) p. 50
Evergreen trees with thick bluish needles, available between November and December for use in Christmas garlands and wreaths but can be bought throughout the year. The fir needles last well in displays. Branches should be stored in the cold, out of water before use.
CARE To condition, cut the stem ends with shears and remove the lower needles. To avoid shedding needles, buy food formulated for Christmas trees.

Achillea 'Moonshine' (**yarrow**)
pp. 42, 78
Tall, summer-flowering perennial with attractive clusters of sulfur-yellow flowers and an aromatic fragrance. The dense flowerheads are useful for filling in arrangements. Cut or purchase the flowers when the flowerheads are at least three-quarters open.
CARE Remove all lower foliage, cut ¹/₃ inch from the stem base, and soak in a solution of flower food.

Alchemilla mollis (**lady's mantle**) p. 88
Perennial plant with lime-green flowers and pretty, fan-shaped leaves that grows to 16–20 inches high. Lady's mantle flowers between early and late summer. The flowers should be cut from the yard or purchased when most of the blossoms are open.
CARE Cut the stem ends cleanly at an angle and then soak in water before using in displays.

Anemone coronaria (**anemone**) p. 38
Jewel-colored flowers in shades of blue, purple, red, and pink, with crowns of leaves around the petals on a leafless stem. Depending on the variety, they grow to 10–18 inches tall. Available from winter to early summer, they peak in spring.
CARE These thirsty flowers require no special treatment. Cut stem ends at an angle and soak in water before use.

Anethum graveolens (**dill**) p. 42
A strongly aromatic herb with feathery flowers that are excellent fillers in

arrangements. Cut or purchase when the main umbel is fully grown.
CARE To condition, cut the stem ends at an angle, remove lower foliage, and place in clean water with flower food.

Anthurium (**anthurium**) p. 78
A tropical plant originating from the rain forests of Colombia, it is prized for its waxy green leaves and brightly colored or pale heart-shaped flowers. The flowers must be mature on purchase and last up to three weeks.
CARE Cut the stem ends and soak in fresh water and flower food. Store out of cold temperatures, which tend to discolor the flowers.

Capsicum (**chili pepper**) p. 42
Chili seeds germinate in spring, and by summer the plants produce shiny red or green fruits. Sold as vegetables for most of the year, dried chili peppers on stems are available in the fall and winter. They are useful for adding color and texture to festive wreaths and garlands.
CARE No special care instructions.

Celosia argentea (**cockscomb**) p. 92
Originally from tropical Africa, this flowering plant comes in two forms, which have either crests or plumes of brilliant deep red, magenta pink, or gold flowers.
CARE Trim the stem ends at an angle and condition with flower food. Remove all foliage.

Centaurea cyanus (**bachelor's buttons**) p. 84
There are many flowers in this family, but the best known are the bright blue annuals with small ruffled petals, available from spring to fall.
CARE Remove the foliage, cut the stem ends at an angle, and place in clean water with flower food.

Clematis vitalba (**clematis vine**) p. 60
Available in fall and winter when the clematis leaves have died back, leaving a vine stem. This vine is ideal for making wreath bases and for wrapping around wreaths and

garlands. Collect from hedges or purchase from specialized florists.
CARE No special care instructions.

Convallaria majalis (**lily-of-the-valley**) p. 84
These sweet-scented, bell-shaped white flowers are available in late spring but can be bought throughout the year at a premium.
CARE Trim the stem ends and place them in water. Do not allow the stems to dry out.

Cymbidium (**cymbidium orchid**) p. 78
These popular orchids come on long or short stems and have waxy flowers in white, yellow, green, or pink.
CARE Cut 1¹/₂ inch off the stem and place in tepid water with flower food. Do not place the flowers in direct sunlight or drafts.

Delphinium 'Blue Bees' (**delphinium**) p. 38
A perennial with tall stems carrying spikes of bell-shaped blue flowers. This variety is often treated before harvesting to make sure it will keep its flowers for up to ten days.
CARE Cut the stems and condition in clean water with flower food.

Echeveria (**succulent**) p. 20
These rosette-shaped succulents originate from Mexico, and there are more than 150 species sold as house and garden plants. They require little water and can survive for weeks in "living wreaths."
CARE Keep the root system intact when lifting from plant pots.

Eustoma grandiflorum (**lisianthus**) pp. 84, 88, 92, 96
These white or blue bell-shaped flowers are arranged on long stems as individual blooms or in panicles.
CARE Cut stem ends and condition in fresh water.

Fagus (**beech**) pp. 46, 88
An attractive green and copper foliage that is most spectacular in fall when the leaves turn rust colored.

CARE Preserve in glycerin for use in displays throughout the year.

Fritillaria pinardii (**fritillary**) p. 84
Delicate, bell-shaped flowers on slender stems, available in spring. This is one of the alpine varieties from Turkey, whose petals are gold on the inside and brown outside. Despite its fragile appearance, it survives well as a cut flower.
CARE Cut the stem ends at an angle and condition with water and flower food.

Galax (**galax**) p. 16
These glossy green heart-shaped leaves are available throughout the year, but turn dark red and mottled in autumn. Most galax leaves are harvested in the Appalachian Mountains and are distributed worldwide.
CARE Buy branches of leaves ready-preserved in glycerin.

Gardenia (**gardenia**) p. 60
Plants with glossy dark green leaves and highly scented waxy white flowers with either single or double blooms.
CARE Gardenias are most commonly sold as house plants and should be kept moist at all times with tepid water. Spray-mist the leaves and condition cut flowers in clean water and flower food before use.

Hedera (**ivy**) pp. 38, 42, 64, 70, 74, 84, 88
This plant has many uses for the flower arranger. Young ivy plants produce trails of lobe-shaped leaves, while mature ivies produce flowers and attractive fruit.
CARE Bunches of fruiting ivy need their stems to be cut and placed in water for a few hours, while young ivy plants in pots should be conditioned overnight with water and flower food.

Helianthus (**sunflower**) p. 42
Originally from the southern and western regions of North America, this annual flower, with its golden-yellow petals and large dark center, has become very fashionable. There are single and double varieties, and it is available in a number of colors as well as the commonly known yellow.
CARE Cut stems at an angle and condition this thirsty flower overnight in fresh water.

Hyacinthus (**hyacinth**) p. 84
An extremely fragrant plant with spikes of bell-shaped flowers in a number of strong and pastel colors. It is popular as a potted bulb plant and now also as a cut flower. The cut flowers last up to 16 days, and each flower stalk can be divided up into individual flowerets and wired into headdresses and bridal bouquets.
CARE Cut stem ends at an angle and wipe away any excess sap.

Hydrangea (**hydrangea**) pp. 56, 64, 88
Another useful flower for arrangers is the long-lasting, large-headed hydrangea. It is available in shades of pink, blue, or white.

CARE As cut flowers, hydrangeas will last for up to ten days but need constant spray-misting with water. If the flowers start to dry out, submerge the flowerheads in water to revive them. They can also be hung up to dry out.

Lavandula (**lavender**) p. 16
This densely growing plant produces fragrant mauve flowers and has beautiful silver-gray stems and leaves. It can be hung up in bunches to dry and then stored and used for projects throughout the year.
CARE When using fresh, remove the lower foliage and place the stems in deep water. Change the water frequently and use flower food.

Leucospermum cordifolium (**pincushion protea**) p. 42
A South African flower commonly known as the pincushion because of its clustered red flowerhead. It lasts well out of water, which makes it a useful flower for hanging garlands.
CARE The woody stems should be cut at an angle and placed in fresh water and flower food.

Lilium (**lily**) p. 64
Large-headed scented lilies such as 'Casablanca' and 'Pompeii' are ideal for wreaths and garlands, as the flowers are long-lasting. To prevent pollen stains when people brush past the display, remove the stamens in the center of the flowerheads.
CARE Cut the stem ends and place in water overnight.

Lonicera (**honeysuckle vine**) pp. 24, 46, 64
Honeysuckle does not last well as a cut flower, but once the leaves have died back in autumn, the flexible vines can be harvested and used to make wreath bases.
CARE No special care instructions.

Ornithogalum montanum (**starflower**) p. 38
This spring-flowering bulb plant has a leafless stem and long-lasting, greenish-white star-shaped flowers.
CARE Cut stem ends and condition for a few hours in clean water before use.

Pittosporum (**pittosporum**) p. 88
Long-lasting evergreen foliage with small ovate leaves; some varieties have variegated leaves.
CARE Cut stem ends cleanly at an angle, then condition in fresh water.

Polianthes tuberosa (**tuberose**) p. 96
Stems of sweetly scented star-shaped cream flowerets that are popular the world over for bridal arrangements.
CARE Cut stem ends cleanly at an angle, and condition in water for a few hours before arranging.

Ranunculus (**ranunculus**) pp. 38, 84
These long-lasting colorful perennials resemble peonies and have either single or double blooms. They are available in winter to late spring.
CARE Cut stems and condition with flower food.

Rosa (**rose**) pp. 16, 56, 88, 92, 96
There is such a wide variety of roses and new shades are always being produced, presenting the flower arranger with a whole host of color combinations and types.
CARE Cut the stem ends at an angle and condition in water and flower food.

Scabiosa (**scabious**) p. 88
Perennial flower available in white and blue. Cut or buy scabious when the flowers are half open.
CARE Place stems in deep water and flower food for a few hours before use.

Scilla (**bluebells**) p. 38
A spring flower found growing wild in woodlands, but it should not be picked from the wild. Both blue and white cultivated hybrids can be bought from florists in spring and will last up to a week in displays.
CARE Cut the stem ends at an angle and soak in fresh water and flower food for a few hours before arranging.

Senecio cineraria (**dusty miller**) p. 96
This attractive silver-gray foliage plant produces clusters of small yellow flowers.
CARE Cut stem ends at an angle and place in lukewarm water for a few hours before arranging.

Stephanandra tanakae (**stephanandra**) p. 78
These arching branches of foliage are available in autumn. The flexible branches are long-lasting and can be twisted around wreath bases to decorative effect.
CARE Cut the stems at an angle and soak in clean water.

Symphoricarpos (**snowberry**) p. 96
Used mainly for their pink and white pearly berries, these are among the first autumn berry plants to appear.
CARE Remove excess leaves and cut the stem ends at an angle before soaking in clean water.

Tropaeolum (**nasturtium**) p. 74
These long-lasting edible flowers have vivid orange or red petals that are used to decorate salads and to make table garlands.
CARE Cut the stem ends at an angle and place them in clean water. Make sure the flowers are free of aphids before use.

Viburnum opulus (**guelder rose**) pp. 38, 56, 88
Lobed deep-green leaves, with fragrant white flowers and clusters of red berries.
CARE Cut stem ends at an angle and place in clean water with flower food.

Viburnum tinus (**viburnum**) p. 92
A very useful plant in winter, when other foliage and flowers are scarce. It produces pink buds and then forms pretty, white, star-shaped flowers between late autumn and early spring. The foliage is available throughout the year for use in displays.
CARE Cut stem ends at an angle and place in clean water with flower food.

suppliers

Wreaths & floral supplies

In addition to the mail-order and specialty sources listed below, see the listing of craft-store chains and check local craft and floral supply shops for wreath forms and floral foam, tools, accessories, and supplies. Purchase live flowers from local flower markets, greengrocers, and supermarkets for the freshest, least expensive, and most varied selection.

FloraCraft
One Longfellow Place
P.O. Box 400
Ludington, MI 49431
616-845-5127
Fax: 616-845-0240
Distributors of wreath, topiary, and geometric forms made of Styrofoam™, extruded foam, and straw; also available are a vast array of floral supplies and accessories.

High Country Floral
P.O. Box 159
Carlton, WA 98814
800-372-2646
Fax: 509-923-2037
Here you can find preserved and stem-dyed wreaths, garlands, and arches; also preserved and stem-dyed baby's-breath in 18 colors, as well as a wide selection of other preserved and dried flowers and leaves, herbs, and spices.

J & T Imports Dried Flowers
P.O. Box 642
Solana Beach, CA 92075
619-481-9781
Available here are all sorts of dried and preserved flowers and foliage, including rosebuds by the pound. While they sell mainly to retail shops, they will fill credit card orders of $50 or more.

Loose Ends
P.O. Box 20310
Keizer, OR 97307
503-390-7457
Here you'll find a wide selection of unusual natural-fiber papers, ribbons, and botanicals, including seagrass, raffia, dried fruits, and fungi.

Maple Ridge Supply
9528 South Bolton Road
Posen, MI 49776
888-881-1880
Metal wreath forms of all sizes and shapes are available from this company. They also make a simple new tool to close the prongs on the forms easily and evenly; it's called the Quik-Crafter™.

May Silk
16202 Distribution Way
Cerritos, CA 90703
800-282-7455
A complete line of silk flowers, plants, foliage, trees, arrangements, and floral accessories is available here.

Nature's Holler
15739 Old Lowery Road North
Omaha, AR 72662
870-426-5489
Suppliers of grapevine wreaths, acorns, pods, pine cones, color-blushed wheat, dried assorted weeds and grasses, baby's-breath, sunflowers, moss, bamboo, wood works—everything you could hope for to make dried arrangements.

Tom Thumb Workshops
14100 Lankford Highway
P.O. Box 357
Mappsville, VA 23407
800-526-6502
Dried and pressed flowers, skeletonized leaves, and craft products can be found here, along with potpourri, herbs, spices, and essential oils.

Craft-store chains

You will be able to find most, if not all, of the supplies called for in this book at any comprehensive craft store near you. Listed below are the largest chains with stores around the country. Call the listed number or use your local Yellow Pages to locate a store in your area. If no instructions are included in the listing, an automated service will ask for your zip code and provide you with the nearest store.

Ben Franklin
There is no centralized number for this franchised chain; look in your local Yellow Pages for the nearest outlet.

Crafts and More
A Division of Ames Department Stores
800-746-7263

Fabri-Centers of America
216-656-2600; ask for Customer Service
This chain operates under different names in different regions of the country. Call and they will locate the affiliate nearest you.

Frank's Nursery and Crafts
313-564-2507; ask for Customer Service

Garden Ridge
281-579-7901; ask for Customer Service

Hobby Lobby
405-745-1100; ask for Customer Service

MJ Designs, Inc.
972-304-2200; ask for Customer Service

Michaels Stores, Inc.
800-642-4235

A. C. Moore
609-228-6700

Old America Stores, L.P.
903-532-3000; ask the operator

Rag Shops, Inc.
973-423-1303; ask for Customer Service

Treasure Island
201-529-1771; press 2 for store locations

Wal-Mart
501-273-4000

Ribbons, ties, & trimmings
Ribbons and decorative cording and other tie trims are widely available in craft, variety, fabric, and sewing notions stores. The sources listed below provide a selection of the more unusual.

Conso Products
P.O. Box 326
Union, SC 29379
800-845-2431
One of the largest distributors of decorative trims, cordings, ropings, tassels, and fringes in various fibers.

Hollywood Trims
A division of the Prym-Dritz Corporation
P.O. Box 5028
Spartanburg, SC 29304
Manufacturers and distributors of rayon, cotton, and metallic trims, cordings, and tassels.

Lion Brand Ribbon
An affiliate of C.M. Offray & Son
Route 24
P.O. Box 601
Chester, NJ 07930
Well-known makers of craft and specialty ribbons of all sorts, including burlap. The ribbons, including wired kinds, come in a broad selection of colors, fabrics, and widths, and are widely available in craft and variety shops as well as floral supply shops.

M & J Trimming Co.
1008 Sixth Avenue
New York, NY 10018
212-391-9072
Has an outstanding collection of decorative trims, cording, ropings, tassels, and fringes in various fibers.

M.P.R. Associates, Inc.
P.O. Box 7343
High Point, NC 27264
800-454-3331
This maker of nontraditional ribbons can provide you with paper lace, corrugated paper ribbons, wired and plain paper and metallic ribbons, paper raffia, and paper twist.

Maxwell · Wellington
811 West Evergreen, Suite 306
Chicago, IL 60622
312-943-2866
Fax: 312-943-9194
Ribbons of paper, velvets, and metallics in a variety of widths are available with or without wires or as luscious handmade bows. Also available are ½-inch colored paper-covered wires to use for stems.

Tinsel Trading Co.
47 West 38th Street
New York, NY 10018
212-730-1030
Offers a unique collection of vintage-to-contemporary trims, tassels, fringes, and cords.

Candles
Candles are widely available in all manner of stores, from supermarkets to gift shops. Listed below are some specialty and mail-order sources. Call for catalogs.

Carolina Candle Co.
P.O. Box 918
Elkin, NC 28621
336-835-6080
A nearly limitless collection of tapers, votives, tea lights, and pillars—scented and unscented—is available from this company. Various aromatherapy candles are also available.

Candlechem Company
32 Thayer Circle
P.O. Box 705
Randolph, MA 02368
781-963-4161; fax: 781-963-3440
Look here for products to make your own candles: basic and designer scents, dyes and pigments, wax additives, novelty, metal, and acrylic molds, waxes, beeswax sheets, equipment, and accessories.

Colonial Candles of Cape Cod
232 Main Street
Hyannis, MA 02601
Mail orders: 800-437-1238, ext. 24
Well-known manufacturer of pillars, hand-dipped tapers, and classic candles in a wide range of colors. If you can't find the color or length you are looking for, call the 800 number.

Miscellaneous
Quality garden tools and accessories are available from the stores listed below or by mail order.

Anthropologie
1801 Walnut Street
Philadelphia, PA 19103
215-564-2313
Good selection of garden accessories, with lots of interesting flowerpots. Nationwide locations; call for one near you.

Colonial Williamsburg
Department 023
P.O. Box 3532
Williamsburg, VA 23187-3532
800-446-9240
Traditional garden accessories. Mail order. Catalog.

Crate & Barrel
P.O. Box 9059
Wheeling, IL 60090-9059
800-451-8217
A wonderful source of good-value china, glass, and plastic containers. Nationwide locations; call for one near you. Mail order. Catalog.

Fiskars Manufacturing Corp.
7811 West Stewart Avenue
Wausau, WI 54401
715-842-2091
Manufacturers of fine-quality scissors, snippers, paper edgers, and punchers, and the very useful all-purpose Craft-Snip, which can be used to cut a variety of heavy-duty materials. They also make excellent tools for gardening and floral work.

Gardener's Eden
P.O. Box 7307
San Francisco, CA 94120-7307
800-822-9600
Quality garden tools and accessories. Nationwide locations; call for one near you. Mail order. Catalog.

Home Depot
Has a wide selection of lumber, outdoor furniture, and plant material at discounted prices. Check your local telephone directory for your nearest store.

Pottery Barn
P.O. Box 7044
San Francisco, CA 94120-7044
800-588-6250
Moderately priced furnishings for indoors and out, including garden furniture, glassware, candlesticks, and hurricane lamps. Nationwide locations; call for one near you. For a catalog call 800-922-5507.

Smith and Hawken
2 Arbor Lane
P.O. Box 6900
Florence, KY 41022-6900
800-776-3336
A wide variety of plants, tools, ornaments, and furniture. Nationwide locations; call for one near you. Mail order. Catalog.

Walnut Hollow
Route 2
Dodgeville, WI 53533
800-395-5995
This company manufactures just about any unfinished wooden shape imaginable, from birdhouses to candle cups.

Wood-N-Crafts, Inc.
P.O. Box 140
Lakeview, MI 48850
800-444-8075
Fax: 517-352-6792
A good source for unfinished wood, such as candlesticks and candle cups, buttons, stars, and hearts.

U.S. Shell, Inc.
P.O. Box 1033
Port Isabel, TX 78578
956-943-1709
Fax: 956-943-6901
Large supplier of packaged shells of all types, from common scallops to rare varieties.

acknowledgments

It has been my great pleasure to work on this book with such an accomplished photographer as James Merrell. James and I have been shooting three books simultaneously to capture all the seasons for each one, and I am extremely grateful to him for bringing his unique blend of good humor, calm intuition, and artistic talent to each day. His patience and endurance are inspirational!

I am also grateful to the extremely artistic and imaginative stylists who have worked on this book, Nato Welton, Martin Bourne, and Margaret Castleton, who have brought their own personal style and expertise to this project. I must also thank the talented illustrator, Helen Smythe, for her superb artworks.

Thank you to the long-suffering staff at Ryland Peters & Small for all their support in the making of this volume, especially Paul Tilby and Zia Mattocks.

I am also grateful to the extremely resourceful and accomplished duo Colin Walton and Bella Pringle, who are so charming and professional to work with.

As always, I am extremely grateful to all my own staff who contributed time and ideas to this book, and also to those who carried on the day-to-day business while I was away. Thanks especially to Ashleigh Hopkins, who continues to support me and manage the business—not to mention her input to the company as a gifted and accomplished florist. In recent years my school has become very popular in Japan, and I am extremely happy to have had the assistance on this project of Shinako Atsumi, Mikiko Tanabe, Hiroko Odakura, Fumiko Inoue, Yoko Okasaki, and Tomoko Akamine. They have all studied with me during the course and have, in their own way, contributed many ideas and suggestions, and have painstakingly created some of the intricate designs.

I am also very grateful to Joan Cardoza for all her help with this book and for her calm and resourceful manner and artistic input. Anita Everard was also called in to help me keep up with James Merrell's speedy photography, and to contribute her immense talent and experience. Thank you also to my personal assistants, Jane Houghton and Sophie Hindley.

A very special thank you to all my colleagues and friends at New Covent Garden Flower Market, especially Dennis Edwards, and all at John Austin & Co. Ltd. Thanks also to Toby at Celestial Buttons, C Best, Something Special, Gerhard Jenne at Konditor & Cook, Jim Brazier, The Peasant Restaurant, Chris Johnson at Sia Parlane, and Peter Lethbridge for their help with this project. Finally, a very personal thank you to Terence Conran for encouraging me to make bigger and better wreaths each Christmas!

credits

Page 10 *Bottom right* striped fabric: Designers Guild.
Page 68 *Bottom right* butterfly fabric: Osborne & Little; fabric butterflies: V V Rouleaux.
Page 91 Marble plates and bowls: David Wainwright.